This flippin' planner belongs to:

_____

CARDINAL BLISS
Planners•Journals•Coloring Books

Welcome to the "Flippin' the bird" flock!

This planner is intended for anyone who gets even a smidgeon of enjoyment from birds. We hope you find yourself smiling as you flip through the days, weeks, and months.

Research shows that birds bring people happiness.

The birds who contributed to the planner & the author did so with the goals of you experiencing droppings of bird happiness while using this planner and find it a useful tool/companion for your own nesting & foraging activities.

Our sincere thanks for taking a flippin' chance on us –

Cardinal Bliss & avian friends
CardinalBlissJournals@gmail.com

CARDINAL BLISS
Planners•Journals•Coloring Books

<u>What's in this flippin' planner♦journal♦logbook:</u>

ISBN Paperback 9798444458365

JANUARY 2022 THROUGH DECEMEBER 2023

January
M	T	W	T	F	S	S
					1	2
3	4	5	6	7	8	9
10	11	12	13	14	15	16
17	18	19	20	21	22	23
24	25	26	27	28	29	30
31						

February
M	T	W	T	F	S	S
	1	2	3	4	5	6
7	8	9	10	11	12	13
14	15	16	17	18	19	20
21	22	23	24	25	26	27
28						

March
M	T	W	T	F	S	S
	1	2	3	4	5	6
7	8	9	10	11	12	13
14	15	16	17	18	19	20
21	22	23	24	25	26	27
28	29	30	31			

July
M	T	W	T	F	S	S
				1	2	3
4	5	6	7	8	9	10
11	12	13	14	15	16	17
18	19	20	21	22	23	24
25	26	27	28	29	30	31

August
M	T	W	T	F	S	S
1	2	3	4	5	6	7
8	9	10	11	12	13	14
15	16	17	18	19	20	21
22	23	24	25	26	27	28
29	30	31				

September
M	T	W	T	F	S	S
			1	2	3	4
5	6	7	8	9	10	11
12	13	14	15	16	17	18
19	20	21	22	23	24	25
26	27	28	29	30		

2023

January
M	T	W	T	F	S	S
						1
2	3	4	5	6	7	8
9	10	11	12	13	14	15
16	17	18	19	20	21	22
23	24	25	26	27	28	29
30	31					

February
M	T	W	T	F	S	S
	1	2	3	4	5	
6	7	8	9	10	11	12
13	14	15	16	17	18	19
20	21	22	23	24	25	26
27	28					

March
M	T	W	T	F	S	S
	1	2	3	4	5	
6	7	8	9	10	11	12
13	14	15	16	17	18	19
20	21	22	23	24	25	26
27	28	29	30	31		

July
M	T	W	T	F	S	S
					1	2
3	4	5	6	7	8	9
10	11	12	13	14	15	16
17	18	19	20	21	22	23
24	25	26	27	28	29	30
31						

August
M	T	W	T	F	S	S
	1	2	3	4	5	6
7	8	9	10	11	12	13
14	15	16	17	18	19	20
21	22	23	24	25	26	27
28	29	30	31			

September
M	T	W	T	F	S	S
				1	2	3
4	5	6	7	8	9	10
11	12	13	14	15	16	17
18	19	20	21	22	23	24
25	26	27	28	29	30	

Notes

_____

_____

_____

_____

_____

TIME FLIES AT A GLANCE

2022

April
M	T	W	T	F	S	S
				1	2	3
4	5	6	7	8	9	10
11	12	13	14	15	16	17
18	19	20	21	22	23	24
25	26	27	28	29	30	

May
M	T	W	T	F	S	S
						1
2	3	4	5	6	7	8
9	10	11	12	13	14	15
16	17	18	19	20	21	22
23	24	25	26	27	28	29
30	31					

June
M	T	W	T	F	S	S
		1	2	3	4	5
6	7	8	9	10	11	12
13	14	15	16	17	18	19
20	21	22	23	24	25	26
27	28	29	30			

October
M	T	W	T	F	S	S
					1	2
3	4	5	6	7	8	9
10	11	12	13	14	15	16
17	18	19	20	21	22	23
24	25	26	27	28	29	30
31						

November
M	T	W	T	F	S	S
	1	2	3	4	5	6
7	8	9	10	11	12	13
14	15	16	17	18	19	20
21	22	23	24	25	26	27
28	29	30				

December
M	T	W	T	F	S	S
			1	2	3	4
5	6	7	8	9	10	11
12	13	14	15	16	17	18
19	20	21	22	23	24	25
26	27	28	29	30	31	

2023

April
M	T	W	T	F	S	S
					1	2
3	4	5	6	7	8	9
10	11	12	13	14	15	16
17	18	19	20	21	22	23
24	25	26	27	28	29	30

May
M	T	W	T	F	S	S
1	2	3	4	5	6	7
8	9	10	11	12	13	14
15	16	17	18	19	20	21
22	23	24	25	26	27	28
29	30	31				

June
M	T	W	T	F	S	S
			1	2	3	4
5	6	7	8	9	10	11
12	13	14	15	16	17	18
19	20	21	22	23	24	25
26	27	28	29	30		

October
M	T	W	T	F	S	S
						1
2	3	4	5	6	7	8
9	10	11	12	13	14	15
16	17	18	19	20	21	22
23	24	25	26	27	28	29
30	31					

November
M	T	W	T	F	S	S
	1	2	3	4	5	
6	7	8	9	10	11	12
13	14	15	16	17	18	19
20	21	22	23	24	25	26
27	28	29	30			

December
M	T	W	T	F	S	S
				1	2	3
4	5	6	7	8	9	10
11	12	13	14	15	16	17
18	19	20	21	22	23	24
25	26	27	28	29	30	31

Notes

JUNE 2022

Sunday	Monday	Tuesday	Wednesday
May 29	May 30	May 31	Jun 1
5	6	7	8
12	13	14	15
19 Father's Day	20	21	22 Rachel Carson Day
26	27	28	29

Thursday	Friday	Saturday	Notes
2	3	4	
9	10	11	
16	17	18	
23	24	25	
30	Jul 1	2	

June 2022

FLIPPPIN' WILD BIRD 411: Intriguing and often humorous names for groups of birds. have been nested throughout this flippin' planner.

We'll start with one of the most well-known flock monikers: A group of crows can be called a murder, congress, horde, muster, or a cauldron.

June

M	T	W	T	F	S	S
		1	2	3	4	5
6	7	8	9	10	11	12
13	14	15	16	17	18	19
20	21	22	23	24	25	26
27	28	29	30			

Monday, May 30

Tuesday, May 30

Wednesday, June 1

Regional/Seasonal Birb Observe-Across the US: Crows are abundant and have a fascinating social structure to observe. The younger crows often stay with their crow family for a few years after fledging and help raise the next couple of generations.

Thursday, June 2

_____
_____
_____
_____
_____
_____
_____
_____

Friday, June 3

_____
_____
_____
_____
_____
_____
_____
_____

Saturday, June 4

_____
_____
_____
_____
_____
_____
_____

Sunday, June 5

_____
_____
_____
_____
_____
_____
_____

June 2022

June

M	T	W	T	F	S	S
		1	2	3	4	5
6	7	8	9	10	11	12
13	14	15	16	17	18	19
20	21	22	23	24	25	26
27	28	29	30			

Monday, June 6

Tuesday, June 7

Wednesday, June 8

Page 10

Beak tweak for the week: What do you call 2,000 mockingbirds? Two kilomockingbirds.

Regional/Seasonal Bird Observe—Across the US:Northern Mockingbirds live year-round. Mockingbirds are backyard dwellers but don't visit feeders. Keep a look out for them on tall shrubs, poles, or utility lines. You may see them hopping over your mowed lawn or on tall shrubs, poles, or utility lines. Listen for its song, which usually mimics numerous other birds at once.
Western US: Sage Thrashers have a breeding season in the intermountain US and winter in Southwest US and Mexico. They look somewhat like washed-out robins.

Thursday, June 9

Friday, June 10

Saturday, June 11

Sunday, June 12

June 2022

FLIPPPIN' WILD BIRD 411:

To bug you. The White-breasted Nuthatch smears blister beetles near the entrance of their nest, which are said to have a repulsive smell.

June

M	T	W	T	F	S	S
		1	2	3	4	5
6	7	8	9	10	11	12
13	14	15	16	17	18	19
20	21	22	23	24	25	26
27	28	29	30			

Monday, June 13

Tuesday, June 14

Wednesday, June 15

Regional/Seasonal Birb Observe—Across the US: White-breasted Nuthatches are a joy to watch climb up and down trees, year-round. They are attracted to nut and suet feeders if you would like to try to entice a Nuthatch into your space.

Thursday, June 16

_____
_____
_____
_____
_____
_____
_____
_____

Friday, June 17

_____
_____
_____
_____
_____
_____
_____
_____

Saturday, June 18

_____
_____
_____
_____
_____
_____
_____
_____

Sunday, June 19

_____
_____
_____
_____
_____
_____
_____

June 2022

FLIPPPIN' WILD BIRD 411:
Hummingbirds are able to remember every flower they have visited in their lifetime & recognize the humans who regularly refill nectar feeders.

June

M	T	W	T	F	S	S
		1	2	3	4	5
6	7	8	9	10	11	12
13	14	15	16	17	18	19
20	21	22	23	24	25	26
27	28	29	30			

Monday, June 20

_____
_____
_____
_____
_____
_____
_____
_____

Tuesday,, June 21

_____
_____
_____
_____
_____
_____
_____

Wednesday, June 22 Rachel Carson Day

_____
_____
_____
_____
_____
_____

Regional/Seasonal Birb Observe—Eastern US: The feisty Ruby-throated Hummingbird is the sole hummingbird to migrate to areas east of the Mississippi for their breeding season over spring and summer.

Western US: Several species of colorful hummingbirds spend their spring and summer breeding season west of the Mississippi.

Thursday, June 23

_____
_____
_____
_____
_____
_____
_____
_____
_____

Friday, June 24

_____
_____
_____
_____
_____
_____
_____
_____

Saturday, June 25

_____
_____
_____
_____
_____
_____
_____
_____

Sunday, June 26

_____
_____
_____
_____
_____
_____
_____
_____

June 2022

This may muster many scolds from the murder of crows when you dare go by or near their congress.

June

M	T	W	T	F	S	S
		1	2	3	4	5
6	7	8	9	10	11	12
13	14	15	16	17	18	19
20	21	22	23	24	25	26
27	28	29	30			

Monday, June 27

_____

_____

_____

_____

_____

_____

_____

_____

Tuesday,, June 28

_____

_____

_____

_____

_____

_____

_____

_____

Wednesday, June 29

_____

_____

_____

_____

_____

_____

_____

<u>Regional/Seasonal Birb Observe</u>—Eastern US: The Ruby-throated Hummingbird is territorial & can be seen dive-bombimg other hummers to keep them away from feeders they are using.
Pacific Northwest: The Rufous Hummingbird guards the flowers and feeders it has chosen as its own with great zeal! It will even chase hummingbirds much bigger than itself from feeders.

Thursday, June 30

_____
_____
_____
_____
_____
_____
_____

Friday, July 1

_____
_____
_____
_____
_____
_____
_____

Saturday, July 2

_____
_____
_____
_____
_____
_____
_____

Sunday, July 3

_____
_____
_____
_____
_____
_____
_____

JULY 2022

Sunday	Monday	Tuesday	Wednesday
26	27	28	29
3	4 Independence Day	5	6
10	11	12	13
17	18	19	20
24 31	25	26	27

Thursday	Friday	Saturday	Notes
30	Jul 1	2	
7	8	9	
14	15	16	
21	22	23	
28	29	30	

July 2022

FLIPPPIN' WILD BIRD 411: A flock of birds of prey is called a cast, cauldron, or kettle.

Eye-popping flips occur in the eagles' dating-mating spiral. Starting high in the sky, a male and female lock talons, spiral down, doing flips & whirls. They break off at the last instant & fly off to avoid crashing. The eagle pair often goes to mate after this spectacular feat. Adolescent eagles practice this with each other.

July

M	T	W	T	F	S	S
				1	2	3
4	5	6	7	8	9	10
11	12	13	14	15	16	17
18	19	20	21	22	23	24
25	26	27	28	29	30	31

Moinday, July 5
Independence Day

_____
_____
_____
_____
_____
_____
_____
_____

Tuesday, July 5

_____
_____
_____
_____
_____
_____

Wednesday, July 6

_____
_____
_____
_____
_____

<u>Beak tweak for the week:</u> What birds go to church?
Birds of prey.

<u>Regional/Seasonal Birb Observe</u>—Across the US: Majestic Bald Eagles winter in tall trees or in cliffs along rivers and lakes. In some pockets of the US, they stay year-round. There are many "eagle cams" one can find on-line in the US to be able to watch an eagle family year after year.

Thursday, July 7

Friday, July 8

Saturday, July 9 910May 30

Sunday, July 10

July 2022

FLIPPPIN' WILD BIRD 411: A flock of Turkey Vultures is called a wake—an apt and darkly humorous description. Turkey Vultures and Buzzards have a keen sense of smell, helping them to locate decomposing carrion.

July

M	T	W	T	F	S	S
				1	2	3
4	5	6	7	8	9	10
11	12	13	14	15	16	17
18	19	20	21	22	23	24
25	26	27	28	29	30	31

Moinday, July 11

Tuesday, July 12

Wednesday, July 13

<u>**Beak tweak for the week:**</u> Why do Vultures get checked in at airports so quickly?   Because they only have carrion.

<u>Regional/Seasonal Birb Observe</u>—Across much of North America: Turkey Vultures can be easily spotted soaring over partly wooded or open land, seeking carrion. One way to discern a Turkey Vulture from a hawk, Turkey Vultures keep their "V" shape while flying, hawks have flat wings.

Thursday, July 14

_____
_____
_____
_____
_____
_____
_____
_____

Friday, July 15

_____
_____
_____
_____
_____
_____
_____
_____

Saturday, July 16

_____
_____
_____
_____
_____
_____
_____

Sunday, July 17

_____
_____
_____
_____
_____
_____
_____

July 2022

An explosive relationship: Male Anna's Hummingbirds hover midair in their courtship display, creating a buzzy song. They fly higher, then dive steeply toward the female. They orient their body with the angle of the sun, drop faster than a jet at full throttle at 9G's, emitting a loud explosive popping sound at the bottom of the dive.

July

M	T	W	T	F	S	S
				1	2	3
4	5	6	7	8	9	10
11	12	13	14	15	16	17
18	19	20	21	22	23	24
25	26	27	28	29	30	31

Moinday, July 18

Tuesday, July 19

Wednesday, July 20

Regional/Seasonal Birb Observe—Pacific Coast: Anna's Hummingbirds live along the coast year-round. They feed on flower nectar and tiny insects. They also enjoy sugar-water mixture in hummingbird feeders. Across the US: All male hummingbirds do diving drops of some sort to impress potential mates.

Thursday, July 21

_____
_____
_____
_____
_____
_____
_____

Friday, July 22

_____
_____
_____
_____
_____
_____
_____

Saturday, July 23

_____
_____
_____
_____
_____
_____
_____

Sunday, July 24

_____
_____
_____
_____
_____
_____
_____

July 2022

A bird's eye takes up about 50 percent of its head. Human eyes take up about 5 percent of person's head. Peoples' eyes would have to be baseball-sized to be proportionate to birds' eyes.

July

M	T	W	T	F	S	S
				1	2	3
4	5	6	7	8	9	10
11	12	13	14	15	16	17
18	19	20	21	22	23	24
25	26	27	28	29	30	31

Moinday, July 25

Tuesday, July 26

Wednesday, July 27

<u>**Beak tweak for the week:**</u> Where do tough birds come from? Hard-boiled eggs.

<u>Regional/Seasonal Birb Observe</u>—Western US, some Northeast US: The brown and tan creeper, blending in with the bark, can be observed starting at the tops of trees and working their way down, foraging in crevices for morsels.

Teen-agers are often observed foraging for morsels.

Thursday, July 28

_____

_____

_____

_____

_____

_____

_____

Friday, July 29

_____

_____

_____

_____

_____

_____

_____

Saturday, July 30

_____

_____

_____

_____

_____

_____

_____

Sunday, July 31

_____

_____

_____

_____

_____

_____

_____

AUGUST 2022

Sunday	Monday	Tuesday	Wednesday
Jul 31	1	2	3
7	8	9	10
14	15	16	17
21	22	23	24
28	29	30	31

Thursday	Friday	Saturday	Notes
4	5	6	
11	12	13	
18	19	20	
25	26	27	
Sep 1	2	3	

August 2022

August

M	T	W	T	F	S	S
1	2	3	4	5	6	7
8	9	10	11	12	13	14
15	16	17	18	19	20	21
22	23	24	25	26	27	28
29	30	31				

Monday, August 1

_____
_____
_____
_____
_____
_____
_____

Tuesday, August 2

_____
_____
_____
_____
_____
_____
_____

Wednesday, August 3

_____
_____
_____
_____
_____
_____

_____

Regional/Seasonal Birb Observe—Across the US: Barn Swallows are sweeping toward and down flyways, migrating toward South America. The Barn Swallows can be identified by their quick, tight turns and dives, lack of gliding, with fluid wing-beats. Males have grayish-blue-black wings.

Thursday, August 4

Friday, August 5

Saturday, August 6

Sunday, August 7

August 2022

FLIPPPIN' WILD BIRD 411: What did you say? Many birds, such as starlings, sing notes too high for humans to hear.

Starlings were brought to the US by Shakespeare enthusiasts in the mid-nineteenth century.

August

M	T	W	T	F	S	S
1	2	3	4	5	6	7
8	9	10	11	12	13	14
15	16	17	18	19	20	21
22	23	24	25	26	27	28
29	30	31				

Monday, August 8

Tuesday, August 9

Wednesday, August 10

Beak tweak for the week: What did the duck physicist say?
Quark, quark.

Regional/Seasonal Birb Observe—Western US: The Sage Thrasher begins
migration from the Intermountain area to the Southwest US and Mexico.
The Eastern US: Has the Brown Thrasher, Northern in the spring and summer,
and Southern year-round. This is an accomplished songbird with more than 1,000
songs.
Across the US: Starlings chase other birds away from backyard feeders.year-round.

Thursday, August 11

_____
_____
_____
_____
_____
_____
_____

Friday, August 12

_____
_____
_____
_____
_____
_____
_____

Saturday, August 13

_____
_____
_____
_____
_____
_____
_____

Sunday, August 14

_____
_____
_____
_____
_____
_____
_____

August 2022

August

M	T	W	T	F	S	S
1	2	3	4	5	6	7
8	9	10	11	12	13	14
15	16	17	18	19	20	21
22	23	24	25	26	27	28
29	30	31				

Monday, August 15

Tuesday, August 16

Wednesday, August 17

Beak tweak for the week: What do you call birds playing hide and seek? Fowl play.

<u>Regional/Seasonal Birb Observe</u>—Southwest US: In the juniper woods, the Juniper Titmouse makes up in personality what they lack in color with their homogenous gray plumage topped off by a cute little gray tuft.
California: The precocious and cute Oak Titmouse makes its home in the Sunshine State.
Eastern US: The Tufted Titmouse lives year-round. Listen for its repeated "peter-peter," call.

Thursday, August 18

Friday, August 19

Saturday, August 20

Sunday, August 21

August 2022

FLIPPPIN' WILD BIRD 411:
That's a pack of pecks! A woodpecker can peck 20 times per second, producing between 10,000 and 12,000 pecks per day. I bet they are tired by sunset.

August

M	T	W	T	F	S	S
1	2	3	4	5	6	7
8	9	10	11	12	13	14
15	16	17	18	19	20	21
22	23	24	25	26	27	28
29	30	31				

Monday, August 22

Tuesday, August 23

Wednesday, August 24

Regional/Seasonal Birb Observe—Across the US, except the Southwest desert: Downy Woodpeckers live where trees grow. They are the smallest North American woodpeckers, abundant and easily spotted with their striking white and black plumage. These cute little guys are attracted to suet feeders and nuts. Their plumage is almost identical to the slightly larger Hairy Woodpecker. Hairy woodpeckers inhabit all of the US, including the Southwest.

Thursday, August 25

Friday, August 26

Saturday, August 27

Sunday, August 28

August 2022

FLIPPPIN' WILD BIRD 411:
You might want to grab a snack. Goldfinch flight calls can be characterized as a bright "per-chick-o-ree" or "potato-chips" delivered in flight. A flock of finches is known as a charm or a trembling. Goldfinch groups are also known as a charm, treasury, vein, rush, and/or trembling.

August

M	T	W	T	F	S	S
1	2	3	4	5	6	7
8	9	10	11	12	13	14
15	16	17	18	19	20	21
22	23	24	25	26	27	28
29	30	31				

Monday, August 29

_____
_____
_____
_____
_____
_____
_____
_____

Tuesday, August 30

_____
_____
_____
_____
_____
_____
_____
_____

Wednesday, August 31

_____
_____
_____
_____
_____
_____
_____
_____

Beak tweak for the week: How many cans does it take to make a bird? Toucans.

Regional/Seasonal Birb Observe—Across the US: American Goldfinches are abundant year-round. The males are bright gold-yellow in the spring, summer, and fall and molt to less colorful plumage for the winter, blending in with the females. Goldfinches are partial to Nyger (thistle) and chipped sunflower seeds.

Thursday, September 1

Friday, Septembe 2

Saturday, September 3

Sunday, September 4

SEPTEMBER 2022

Sunday	Monday	Tuesday	Wednesday
28	29	30	31
4	5 Labor Day	6	7
11	12	13	14
18	19	20	21
25	26	27	28

Thursday	Friday	Saturday	Notes
Sep 1	2	3	
8	9	10	
15	16	17	
22	23	24	
29	30	Oct 1	

September 2022

September

M	T	W	T	F	S	S
			1	2	3	4
5	6	7	8	9	10	11
12	13	14	15	16	17	18
19	20	21	22	23	24	25
26	27	28	29	30		

Monday, September 5 - Labor Day

Tuesday, September 6

Wednesday, September 7

<u>**Beak tweak for the week**</u>: Who is a penguin's favorite relative?   Aunt Artica.

<u>Regional/Seasonal Birb Observe:</u> Across the US: Robins, thought of as a harbinger of spring, often stay at their breeding ground year-round. In the winter, they are not seen on the grass because they are roosting in trees.

Nighthawks are swooping through the US toward & on flyways in their early September migration. They use river valleys to navigate. It is worth the spectacle to find "Nighthawk Searches" through your local Audobon Society.

Thursday, September 8

_____
_____
_____
_____
_____
_____
_____
_____
_____

Friday, September 9

_____
_____
_____
_____
_____
_____
_____
_____

Saturday, September 10

_____
_____
_____
_____
_____
_____
_____
_____

Sunday, September 11

_____
_____
_____
_____
_____
_____
_____
_____

September 2022

September

M	T	W	T	F	S	S
			1	2	3	4
5	6	7	8	9	10	11
12	13	14	15	16	17	18
19	20	21	22	23	24	25
26	27	28	29	30		

Monday, September 12

Tuesday, September 13

Wednesday, September 14

<u>**Beak tweak for the week:**</u> What do you call a rude bird? A mockingbird.

<u>Regional/Seasonal Birb Observe</u>-Flipping off those indoor and outdoor light switches, midnight to 6am, spring and fall, helps to keep our hard-flying avian friends on course during their migratory flights, by decreasing confusing light sources.

Thursday, September 15

Friday, September 16

Saturday, September 17

Sunday, September 18

September 2022

Rufous hummingbirds will fight any other hummingbird, even Southwest hummers twice its size, for flowers and feeders.

These fierce little fighters usually win.

September

M	T	W	T	F	S	S
			1	2	3	4
5	6	7	8	9	10	11
12	13	14	15	16	17	18
19	20	21	22	23	24	25
26	27	28	29	30		

Monday, September 19

Tuesday, September 20

Wednesday, September 21

<u>Beak tweak for the week:</u> My uncle named his little crow with soft feathers Microwsoft.

<u>Regional/Seasonal Birb Observe</u>—Rocky Mountains: The courageous Rufous Hummingbird spends fall in the Rockies. They are known to be relentless attackers at flowers and feeders. They breed the furthest North of any hummingbird.
Across the US: Hummingbirds are traveling solo to warmer climates. If you keep your feeders clean and stocked with fresh nectar for hummingbird travelers, they will remember you (yes, you) & your location the following year.

Thursday, September 22

_____
_____
_____
_____
_____
_____
_____
_____

Friday, September 23

_____
_____
_____
_____
_____
_____
_____

Saturday, September 24

_____
_____
_____
_____
_____
_____
_____

Sunday, September 25

_____
_____
_____
_____
_____
_____
_____

September 2022

September

M	T	W	T	F	S	S
			1	2	3	4
5	6	7	8	9	10	11
12	13	14	15	16	17	18
19	20	21	22	23	24	25
26	27	28	29	30		

Monday, September 26

_____
_____
_____
_____
_____
_____
_____
_____

Tuesday, September 27

_____
_____
_____
_____
_____
_____
_____
_____

Wednesday, September 28

_____
_____
_____
_____
_____
_____
_____

<u>**Beak tweak for the week:**</u> What did the mouse say when they walked into the bar full of hawks? This is hawkward.

<u>Regional/Seasonal Birb Observe</u>—Across the US: Various species of hawks are migrating south for the winter. They fly in the daylight.

There are hawk-watching stations dotted all through the US. Several hawks may be spotted in one day, if not hundreds, during migration. Your local Audobon Society should have a list of nearby hawk-watching stations.

Thursday, September 29

Friday, September 30

Saturday, October 1

Sunday, October 2

OCTOBER 2022

Sunday	Monday	Tuesday	Wednesday
25	26	27	28
2	3	4	5
9	10	11	12
16	17	18	19
23 / 30	24 / Halloween 31	25	26

Thursday	Friday	Saturday	Notes
29	30	Oct 1	
6	7	8	
13	14	15	
20	21	22	
27	28	29	

October 2022

FLIPPIN' WILD BIRD 411:

Jamming gams: Owls have long legs often hidden by their posture, body shape, and feathers. Owl talons are incredibly strong for hunting, Owl legs are long to keep their eyes safe from the scratches of their prey. We usually only see owl toes from beneath their feathers.

October						
M	T	W	T	F	S	S
					1	2
3	4	5	6	7	8	9
10	11	12	13	14	15	16
17	18	19	20	21	22	23
24	25	26	27	28	29	30
31						

Monday, October 3

_____
_____
_____
_____
_____
_____
_____

Tuesday, October 4

_____
_____
_____
_____
_____
_____
_____

Wednesday, October 5

_____
_____
_____
_____
_____
_____

Regional/Seasonal Birb Observe—Owls are found on every continent but Antarctica. Owls are active at night, while they hunt nocturnal prey, using silent flight. To spot an owl listen for their calls and follow with good set of binoculars, looking for their shapes moving in the dark. Owls prefer dense trees abutting clearings. Tree-lined cemeteries are often terrific places to locate owls.

Thursday, October 6

Friday, October 7

Saturday, October 8

Sunday, October 9

October 2022

October

M	T	W	T	F	S	S
					1	2
3	4	5	6	7	8	9
10	11	12	13	14	15	16
17	18	19	20	21	22	23
24	25	26	27	28	29	30
31						

Monday, October 10

_____
_____
_____
_____
_____
_____
_____

Tuesday, October 11

_____
_____
_____
_____
_____
_____
_____

Wednesday, October 12

_____
_____
_____
_____
_____
_____

<u>Regional/Seasonal Birb Observe</u>—Across the US year-round: Lives the quintessential owl of legend, the Great Horned Owl, with its deep hoots adding to the atmosphere of the night.

Thursday, October 13

Friday, October 14

Saturday, October 15

Sunday, October 16

October 2022

A wise, studious, glaring owl, indeed.

October

M	T	W	T	F	S	S
					1	2
3	4	5	6	7	8	9
10	11	12	13	14	15	16
17	18	19	20	21	22	23
24	25	26	27	28	29	30
31						

Monday, October 17

_____
_____
_____
_____
_____
_____
_____

Tuesday, October 18

_____
_____
_____
_____
_____
_____
_____

Wednesday, October 19

_____
_____
_____
_____
_____
_____

_____

<u>Regional/Seasonal Birb Observe</u>—The Eastern US: Year-round Barred Owls treat listeners to their classic owl hoots.

The Western US: Year-round, the hollow hoots, rather than screeches, of the Western Screech Owl, a formidable hunter, can be heard. These owls camouflage with trees by backing against the bark.

Thursday, October 20

_____
_____
_____
_____
_____
_____
_____

Friday, October 21

_____
_____
_____
_____
_____
_____
_____
_____

Saturday, October 22

_____
_____
_____
_____
_____
_____
_____
_____

Sunday, October 23

_____
_____
_____
_____
_____
_____
_____

October 2022

The barn owl's hearing is so precise that it can strike prey in total darkness. Barn owls, with their ghostly faces, attraction to church steeples and belfries, and their blood-curdling scream, have become woven into legend and superstition.

October

M	T	W	T	F	S	S
					1	2
3	4	5	6	7	8	9
10	11	12	13	14	15	16
17	18	19	20	21	22	23
24	25	26	27	28	29	30
31						

Monday, October 24

_____
_____
_____
_____
_____
_____
_____
_____

Tuesday, October 25

_____
_____
_____
_____
_____
_____
_____
_____

Wednesday, October 26

_____
_____
_____
_____
_____
_____

Regional/Seasonal Birb Observe—Western US: Year-round Barn Owls are abundant, except in a few pockets.
Eastern US: Barn owls live year-round but are not as common.

Eastern US: The blood-chilling call of Eastern Screech-owl haunts wooded areas year-round.

Thursday, October 27

_____
_____
_____
_____
_____
_____
_____

Friday, October 28

_____
_____
_____
_____
_____
_____
_____

Saturday, October 29

_____
_____
_____
_____
_____
_____

Sunday, October 30

_____
_____
_____
_____
_____
_____

October 2022

FLIPPPIN' WILD BIRD 411:
The haunting owl. The owl is referred to as the ringer of the bell for the murder of Macbeth by Shakespeare, "Fatal Bellman" in "Comedy of Errors" rubbing wings with goblins and sprites.

October

M	T	W	T	F	S	S
					1	2
3	4	5	6	7	8	9
10	11	12	13	14	15	16
17	18	19	20	21	22	23
24	25	26	27	28	29	30
31						

Monday, October 31
Halloween

_____
_____
_____
_____
_____
_____

Tuesday, November 1

_____
_____
_____
_____
_____
_____
_____

Wednesday, November 2

_____
_____
_____
_____
_____
_____

<u>Regional/Seasonal Birb Observe—</u>
Across the US: Hooting season begins in late fall. Owl hoots
do increase in number. Owls call as they establish and defend
territories. Owl calls are also part of courtship displays and they do
mate for life.

Thursday, November 3

_____
_____
_____
_____
_____
_____
_____

Friday, November 4

_____
_____
_____
_____
_____
_____
_____
_____

Saturday, November 6

_____
_____
_____
_____
_____
_____
_____

Sunday, November 7

_____
_____
_____
_____
_____
_____
_____

NOVEMBER 2022

Sunday	Monday	Tuesday	Wednesday
30 Oct	31 Oct Halloween	Nov 1	2
6	7	8	9
13	14	15	16
20	21	22	23
27	28	29	30

Thursday	Friday	Saturday	Notes
3	4	5	
10	11	12	
17	18	19	
24 Thanksgiving	25	26	
Dec 1	Dec 2	Dec 3	

November 2022

Burrowing Owls carpet the entrance of their homes with animal dung to attract dung beetles and other insects to eat while nesting. They also collect bottle caps, cigarette butts, gum wrappers, and other bits to line the entrance to signify the borrow is occupied.

November

M	T	W	T	F	S	S
	1	2	3	4	5	6
7	8	9	10	11	12	13
14	15	16	17	18	19	20
21	22	23	24	25	26	27
28	29	30				

Monday, November 7

_____
_____
_____
_____
_____
_____
_____

Tuesday, November 8

_____
_____
_____
_____
_____
_____
_____

Wednesday, November 9

_____
_____
_____
_____
_____
_____

Regional/Seasonal Birb Observe—Grasslands of the US: With patience,
Burrowing Owls can be spotted while they are out and standing on
their long legs to hunt. They are well-camouflaged with the land and
may look like moving mounds of dirt. Early morning or evening is the
best time to catch a glimpse of this cute and curious owl.

Thursday, November 10

Friday, November 11

Saturday, November 12

Sunday, November 13

November 2022

November

M	T	W	T	F	S	S
	1	2	3	4	5	6
7	8	9	10	11	12	13
14	15	16	17	18	19	20
21	22	23	24	25	26	27
28	29	30				

Monday, November 14

_____
_____
_____
_____
_____
_____
_____

Tuesday, November 15

_____
_____
_____
_____
_____
_____
_____

Wednesday, November 6

_____
_____
_____
_____
_____
_____

Regional/Seasonal Birb Observe—Across the US: The Red-Breasted Nuthatch may be noted during the winter. As these are friendly and bold birds, patient backyard birders may find the nuthatches hand-feeding from them.

Thursday, November 17

_____
_____
_____
_____
_____
_____
_____
_____

Friday, November 18

_____
_____
_____
_____
_____
_____
_____
_____

Saturday, November 19

_____
_____
_____
_____
_____
_____
_____
_____

Sunday, November 20

_____
_____
_____
_____
_____
_____
_____
_____

November 2022

November

M	T	W	T	F	S	S
	1	2	3	4	5	6
7	8	9	10	11	12	13
14	15	16	17	18	19	20
21	22	23	24	25	26	27
28	29	30				

Monday, November 21

_____
_____
_____
_____
_____
_____
_____

Tuesday, November 22

_____
_____
_____
_____
_____
_____
_____

Wednesday, November 23

_____
_____
_____
_____
_____

Regional/Seasonal Birb Observe—Across the US: Owls start nesting earlier than other birds so their young are ready to learn to fly and hunt prey by spring, when the weather is warmer, and prey is abundant. The following fall, young owls are chased from the nest as new adults to establish their own territory.

Thursday, November 24 Thanksgiving

Friday, November 25

Saturday, November 26

Sunday, November 27

November 2022

November

M	T	W	T	F	S	S
	1	2	3	4	5	6
7	8	9	10	11	12	13
14	15	16	17	18	19	20
21	22	23	24	25	26	27
28	29	30				

Monday, November 28

Tuesday, November 29

Wednesday, November 30

Regional/Seasonal Birb Observe—Across the US except in a few Northwest pockets: Wild Turkeys can be found year-round strolling and forging over in wooded areas (with males gobbling and females purring).

Thursday, December 1

Friday, December 2

Saturday, December 3

Sunday, December 4

DECEMBER 2022

Sunday	Monday	Tuesday	Wednesday
Nov 27	Nov 28	Nov 29	Nov 30
4	5	6	7
11	12	13	14
18 Hanukkha begins	19	20	21
25 Christmas Day	26 Kwanza begins	27	28

Thursday	Friday	Saturday	Notes
Dec 1	2	3	
8	9	10	
15	16	17	
22	23	24 Christmas Eve	
29	30	31 New Year's Eve	

December 2022

A bird's feathers weigh more than its skeleton.

December

M	T	W	T	F	S	S
			1	2	3	4
5	6	7	8	9	10	11
12	13	14	15	16	17	18
19	20	21	22	23	24	25
26	27	28	29	30	31	

Monday, December 5

_____
_____
_____
_____
_____
_____
_____

Tuesday, December 6

_____
_____
_____
_____
_____
_____
_____

Wednesday, December 7

_____
_____
_____
_____
_____
_____

Regional/Seasonal Birb Observe—Central and Southeastern US:
Yellow-Rumped Warblers spend winter here and in Mexico. Also known as
"butter-butts," their plumage is not as brilliant in the winter.

Thursday, December 8

Friday, December 9

Saturday, December 10

Sunday, December 11

December 2022

Clark's Nutcrackers hide thousands of seeds each year. They have an incredible memory for the location of their caches. Many pines of the Northwest depend on the Nutcrackers for propogartion by dispersing seeds. Nutcrackers can breed early during the harsh winter, feeding nestlings from their caches.

December

M	T	W	T	F	S	S
			1	2	3	4
5	6	7	8	9	10	11
12	13	14	15	16	17	18
19	20	21	22	23	24	25
26	27	28	29	30	31	

Monday, December 12

_____
_____
_____
_____
_____
_____
_____
_____

Tuesday, December 13

_____
_____
_____
_____
_____
_____
_____
_____

Wednesday, December 14

_____
_____
_____
_____
_____
_____
_____

Regional/Seasonal Birb Observe—US West mountains, year-round: The Clark's Nutcracker is abundant in forests, campgrounds, national parks. Keep an ear out for their long calls.
Eastern US: The Northen Cardinal is abundant and brilliant, with imales and their deep red coloring   females with their rich olive brown and crimson coloring.

Thursday, December 15

_____
_____
_____
_____
_____
_____
_____

Friday, December 16

_____
_____
_____
_____
_____
_____
_____

Saturday, December 17

_____
_____
_____
_____
_____
_____
_____

Sunday, December 18 Hanuakka begins

_____
_____
_____
_____
_____
_____
_____

December 2022

December

M	T	W	T	F	S	S
			1	2	3	4
5	6	7	8	9	10	11
12	13	14	15	16	17	18
19	20	21	22	23	24	25
26	27	28	29	30	31	

Monday, December 19

_____
_____
_____
_____
_____
_____
_____

Tuesday, December 20

_____
_____
_____
_____
_____
_____
_____

Wednesday, December 21

_____
_____
_____
_____
_____
_____
_____

Regional/Seasonal Birb Observe—Across most of the US: During cold nights and bad weather Chickadees will roost alone in any little pocket or crevice they can find: trees, cracks in buildings, roosting pockets or bird boxes.

Thursday, December 22

_____
_____
_____
_____
_____
_____
_____
_____

Friday, December 23

_____
_____
_____
_____
_____
_____
_____
_____

Saturday, Dec 24 Christmas Eve

_____
_____
_____
_____
_____
_____
_____

Sunday, Dec 25 Christmas Day

_____
_____
_____
_____
_____
_____
_____

December 2022

December

M	T	W	T	F	S	S
			1	2	3	4
5	6	7	8	9	10	11
12	13	14	15	16	17	18
19	20	21	22	23	24	25
26	27	28	29	30	31	

Mon, Dec 26 Kwanza begins

_____
_____
_____
_____
_____
_____
_____

Tuesday, December 27

_____
_____
_____
_____
_____
_____
_____

Wednesday, December 28

_____
_____
_____
_____
_____
_____

Beak tweak for the week: What kind of bird robs you while you bathe? A robber duck.

Regional/Seasonal Birb Observe—In cold regions of the US: A heated birdbath will attract many wintering birds to your yard, patio or balcony.

Thursday, December 29

_____
_____
_____
_____
_____
_____
_____

Friday, December 30

_____
_____
_____
_____
_____
_____
_____

Sat, Dec 31 New Year's Eve

_____
_____
_____
_____
_____
_____
_____

Sunday, Jan 1 New Year's Day

_____
_____
_____
_____
_____
_____
_____

JANUARY 2023

Sunday	Monday	Tuesday	Wednesday
1 New Year's Day	2	3	4
8	9	10	11
15	16 Martin Luther King Day	17	18
22	23	24	25
29	30	31	Feb 1

Thursday	Friday	Saturday	Notes
5	6	7	
12	13	14	
19	20	21	
26	27	28	
Feb 2	Feb 3	Feb 4	

January 2023

You'll find my food nevermore! Ravens are known to hide their food in one place when in the sight of another raven. Once unobserved, they will move their cache to a new spot.

January

M	T	W	T	F	S	S
						1
2	3	4	5	6	7	8
9	10	11	12	13	14	15
16	17	18	19	20	21	22
23	24	25	26	27	28	29
30	31					

Monday, January 2

_____
_____
_____
_____
_____
_____
_____

Tuesday, January 3

_____
_____
_____
_____
_____
_____
_____

Wednesday, January 4

_____
_____
_____
_____
_____
_____

_____

<u>**Beak tweak for the week:**</u> What do you call a gathering of crows and ravens? A murder conspiracy.

<u>Regional/Seasonal Birb Observe:</u> Ravens live on every continent but the Antarctic.

Some Ravens make their home year-round in the Arctic—it's in black and white.

Thursday, January 5

Friday, January 6

Saturday, January 7

Sunday, January 8

January 2023

<u>FLIPPPIN' WILD BIRD</u> <u>411</u>: A group of Waxwings is collectively known as an "ear-full" and a "museum" of waxwings.

Red, waxy secretions found on the wingtips of waxwings give them their name.

January

M	T	W	T	F	S	S
						1
2	3	4	5	6	7	8
9	10	11	12	13	14	15
16	17	18	19	20	21	22
23	24	25	26	27	28	29
30	31					

Monday, January 9

_____
_____
_____
_____
_____
_____
_____

Tuesday, January 10

_____
_____
_____
_____
_____
_____
_____

Wednesday, January 11

_____
_____
_____
_____
_____
_____

Beak tweak for the week: I saw two people fencing at a wax museum, Madam Two-swords.

Regional/Seasonal Birb Observe—Northwest US and Northern Rocky
Mountain Region: Bohemian Waxwings live year-round.
Across the Northern US: Cedar Waxwings make their home year-round.
Across the Southern US: Many Cedar Waxwings enjoy the warmer
weather during the winter.

Thursday, January 12

_____
_____
_____
_____
_____
_____
_____

Friday, January 13

_____
_____
_____
_____
_____
_____
_____

Saturday, January 14

_____
_____
_____
_____
_____
_____
_____

Sunday, January 15

_____
_____
_____
_____
_____
_____
_____

January 2023

FLIPPPIN' WILD BIRD 411: Time for a catnap, umm, bird nap Sooty Terns take 1 to 2-second naps while flying out at sea because they have nowhere to land. Talk about flying blind. Sooty terns are social tropical sea birds, and their nesting colonies are known to be so noisy that OSHA limits worker time in a colony to 30 minutes.

January

M	T	W	T	F	S	S
						1
2	3	4	5	6	7	8
9	10	11	12	13	14	15
16	17	18	19	20	21	22
23	24	25	26	27	28	29
30	31					

Mon, Jan 16 Martin Luther King Day

_____
_____
_____
_____
_____
_____
_____

Tuesday, January 17

_____
_____
_____
_____
_____
_____
_____

Wednesday, January 18

_____
_____
_____
_____
_____
_____

Regional/Seasonal Birb Observe—Across the US: Cute, fluffy, Dark-Eyed Juncos, also known as "snowbirds," can be spotted all over the US in the winter months, flittering about on the ground and making ticking calls. The eastern US Drak-Eyed Juncos are gray with a white breast. Out west, the Dark-Eyed Juncos have several color varations. They are all cute and are fans of red and/or white proso millet & cracked corn.

Thursday, January 19

Friday, January 20

Saturday, January 21

Sunday, January 22

January 2023

January

M	T	W	T	F	S	S
						1
2	3	4	5	6	7	8
9	10	11	12	13	14	15
16	17	18	19	20	21	22
23	24	25	26	27	28	29
30	31					

Monday, January 23

Tuesday, January 24

Wednesday, January 25

Beak tweak for the week: What kind of transgression is it when you can't identify a red bird?   A cardinal sin.

Regional/Seasonal Birb Observe—Across the US, in cold areas: Cardinals roost together in conifers on cold winter nights and in bad weather.

Thursday, January 26

Friday, January 27

Saturday, January 28

Sunday, January 29

January 2023

FLIPPPIN' WILD BIRD 411: Male Snow-Buntings flip colors from brownish to snow-white when they rub their heads and bellies on the snow. Snow buntings are often called snowflakes with fluffy white plumage and continual restlessness, appearing to be flurrying. Snow Bunting males bring food to the brooding females every 15 minutes or so, since the females hardly ever leave the nest.

January

M	T	W	T	F	S	S
						1
2	3	4	5	6	7	8
9	10	11	12	13	14	15
16	17	18	19	20	21	22
23	24	25	26	27	28	29
30	31					

Monday, January 30

_____
_____
_____
_____
_____
_____
_____

Tuesday, January 31

_____
_____
_____
_____
_____
_____
_____

Wednesday, Fenbruary 1

_____
_____
_____
_____
_____
_____
_____

Regional/Seasonal Birb Observe— Across the US: Downy woodpeckers inhabit backyards across the US in all seasons. In the winter, they enjoy suet and nuts.

Thursday, Fenbruary 2

_____
_____
_____
_____
_____
_____
_____
_____

Friday, Fenbruary 3

_____
_____
_____
_____
_____
_____
_____
_____

Saturday, Fenbruary 4

_____
_____
_____
_____
_____
_____
_____
_____

Sunday, Fenbruary 5

_____
_____
_____
_____
_____
_____
_____
_____

FEBRUARY 2023

Sunday	Monday	Tuesday	Wednesday
Jan 29	Jan 30	Jan 31	Feb 1
5	6	7	8
12	13	14 Valentine's Day	15
19	20 President's Day	21	22
26	27	28	Mar 1

Thursday	Friday	Saturday	Notes
2	3	4	
9	10	11	
16	17	18	
23	24	25	
Mar 2	Mar 3	Mar 4	

February 2023

Woodpeckers can identify each other by the drumming sound. Woodpeckers drum on all sorts of structures, much to the chagrin of some human neighbors.

February

M	T	W	T	F	S	S
		1	2	3	4	5
6	7	8	9	10	11	12
13	14	15	16	17	18	19
20	21	22	23	24	25	26
27	28					

Monday, Fenbruary 6

_____
_____
_____
_____
_____
_____
_____

Tuesday, Fenbruary 7

_____
_____
_____
_____
_____
_____
_____

Wednesday, February 8

_____
_____
_____
_____
_____
_____
_____

<u>Regional/Seasonal Birb Observe</u>—Across the US: Incredibly adorable Downy Woodpeckers inhabit backyards across the US in all seasons. In the winter, they can be attracted to backyards with suet and nuts. The Hairy Woodpecker looks like a bigger version of the Downy Woodpecker.

Thursday, February 9

_____
_____
_____
_____
_____
_____
_____

Friday, February 10

_____
_____
_____
_____
_____
_____
_____

Saturday, February 11

_____
_____
_____
_____
_____
_____
_____

Sunday, February 12

_____
_____
_____
_____
_____
_____
_____

February 2023

A flock of blue jays is knowns as a band, party, scold, cast.

Do they have cast parties with a band? The Blue Jay's fondness for acorns is credited with helping spread oak tree after the last glacial period.

February

M	T	W	T	F	S	S
		1	2	3	4	5
6	7	8	9	10	11	12
13	14	15	16	17	18	19
20	21	22	23	24	25	26
27	28					

Monday, Fenbruary 13

Tuesday, Fenbruary 14 Valentine's Day

Wednesday, February 15

<u>Beak tweak for the week:</u> Why did the chicken cross the playground?   Because it wanted to get to the other slide.

<u>Regional/Seasonal Birb Observe</u>—Central and Eastern US: Blue Jays live year-round. One can enjoy observing their teamwork.
Northwest: Blue Jays can entertain observers during the Fall and Winter. Only 1 percent of bluejays were found with remains of eggs or other birds in their stomachs, dispelling the belief that such is typical food for the Jay.

Thursday, February 16

Friday, February 17

Saturday, February 18

Sunday, February 19

February 2023

American Robins have super-power eyesight enabling them to see minute disturbances in the soil, detecting where worms are moving.

Put a ring on it. Male robins have a white ring marking around their eyes, and females do not.

February

M	T	W	T	F	S	S
		1	2	3	4	5
6	7	8	9	10	11	12
13	14	15	16	17	18	19
20	21	22	23	24	25	26
27	28					

Monday, Feb 20 Presidents' Day

_____

Tuesday, February 21

_____

Wednesday, February 22

_____

Regional/Seasonal Birb Observe—Across the US: Robins can be spotted on the ground, spring through the fall. In the winter, they roost in trees — which is why Robins appear scarce in winter. They don't typically migrate.

Thursday, February 23

Friday, February 24

Saturday, February 25

Sunday, February 26

February 2023

Sapsuckers are part of the woodpecker family

February

M	T	W	T	F	S	S
		1	2	3	4	5
6	7	8	9	10	11	12
13	14	15	16	17	18	19
20	21	22	23	24	25	26
27	28					

Monday, February 27

_____
_____
_____
_____
_____
_____
_____

Tuesday, February 28

_____
_____
_____
_____
_____
_____
_____

Wednesday, March 1

_____
_____
_____
_____
_____
_____
_____

<u>**Beak tweak for the week:**</u> What do you call a trader who tries to take over all of the ramen stock? Uslurper.

<u>**Regional/Seasonal Birb Observe**</u>—Eastern US: Yellow-Bellied Sap-Suckers are often migratory. Their sap wells can be easily identified as holes in a straight row on several trees. Sap-Suckers can often be spotted tending to their sap wells. In spring, listen for their mewing calls and their distinctive, irregular drumming.
Western US: The Red-Naped Sap-Sucker lives here year-round.
Pacific Coast of the US: The Red-Breasted Sap-Sucker calls this home year-round.
Western US: The Red-Naped Sap-Sucker makes their home here year-round.
<u>Pacific Coast of the US: The Red-Breasted Sap-Sucker calls this home year-round.</u>

Thursday, March 2

Friday, March 3

Saturday, March 4

Sunday, March 5

MARCH 2023

Sunday	Monday	Tuesday	Wednesday
Feb 26	Feb 27	Feb 28	1
5	6	7	8
12	13	14	15
19	20	21	22
26	27	28	29

Thursday	Friday	Saturday	Notes
2	3	4	
9	10	11	
16	17 St. Patrick's Day	18	
23	24	25	
30	31	Apr 1	

March 2023

FLIPPPIN' WILD BIRD 411:
Ruby-throated Hummingbirds time their migration into Canada to coincide with the arrival of slurps of Sapsuckers. The hummers can take advantage of easy access to sap.

March

M	T	W	T	F	S	S
		1	2	3	4	5
6	7	8	9	10	11	12
13	14	15	16	17	18	19
20	21	22	23	24	25	26
27	28	29	30	31		

Monday, March 6

Tuesday, March 7

Wednesday, March 8

<u>**Beak tweak for the week:**</u> What is the most musical SUV?
The Hummer.

<u>Regional/Seasonal Birb Observe</u>—Southern US: First arrivals of hummingbirds are filtering in. The numbers of hummers in the southern US build-up through April in areas where nectar is easy to find.

Thursday, March 9

Friday, March 10

Saturday, March 11

Sunday, March 12

March 2023

FLIPPPIN' WILD BIRD 411: Ovenbirds, a warbler, migrate with storm fronts on their spring and fall migration routes. They are also known as "Rock Star Birds" because of their "Rock Star" walk.

March

M	T	W	T	F	S	S
		1	2	3	4	5
6	7	8	9	10	11	12
13	14	15	16	17	18	19
20	21	22	23	24	25	26
27	28	29	30	31		

Monday, March 13

_____
_____
_____
_____
_____
_____
_____

Tuesday, March 14

_____
_____
_____
_____
_____
_____
_____

Wednesday, March 15

_____
_____
_____
_____
_____
_____
_____

Beak tweak for the week: Don't be upset with the hall light switch that keeps shocking you. It's reminding you of your potential.

<u>Regional/Seasonal Birb Observe</u>—Flipping off those indoor and outdoor light switches, midnight to 6a, spring, and fall, helps keep our hard-flying avian friends on course, by decreasing confusing light sources.

Thursday, March 16

_____
_____
_____
_____
_____
_____
_____
_____

Friday, March 17 St. Patrick's Day

_____
_____
_____
_____
_____
_____
_____
_____

Saturday, March 18

_____
_____
_____
_____
_____
_____
_____

Sunday, March 19

_____
_____
_____
_____
_____
_____
_____

March 2023

FLIPPIN' WILD BIRD 411:
A flock of starlings may be called chattering, affliction, murmuration, scourge, constellation.

Scourage and affliction are appropriate monikers.

March

M	T	W	T	F	S	S
		1	2	3	4	5
6	7	8	9	10	11	12
13	14	15	16	17	18	19
20	21	22	23	24	25	26
27	28	29	30	31		

Monday, March 20

_____
_____
_____
_____
_____
_____
_____

Tuesday, March 21

_____
_____
_____
_____
_____
_____
_____

Wednesday, March 22

_____
_____
_____
_____
_____
_____

_____

<u>Beak tweak for the week:</u> I have an affliction where I am compelled to tell bad jokes about dolphins. I don't do it on porpoise.

<u>Regional/Seasonal Birb Observe</u>—For BirdNerds: Colorado State University and the Cornell Lab of Ornithology "BirdCast" Bird migration forecast maps show predicted nocturnal migration 3 hours after local sunset and are updated every 6 hours.

https://birdcast.info

Thursday, March 23

Friday, March 24

Saturday, March 25

Sunday, March 26

March 2023

FLIPPPIN' WILD BIRD 411: Chimney Swifts remain almost entirely airborne. They cannot land or perch. They cling to the inside of chimneys or other vertical structures with their long claws. During migration, thousands of swifts roost together in chimneys, funneling into them in awe-striking tornado-like flocks at dusk. Chimney Swifts are masters of catching insects mid-flight—their primary food source. People have adopted building fake chimneys around the US to provide homes for these phenomenal insect predators.

March

M	T	W	T	F	S	S
		1	2	3	4	5
6	7	8	9	10	11	12
13	14	15	16	17	18	19
20	21	22	23	24	25	26
27	28	29	30	31		

Monday, March 27

Tuesday, March 28

Wednesday, March 29

Beak tweak for the week: My friend is super busy as a chimney sweep - business is through the roof.

Regional/Seasonal Birb Observe—Eastern and Northern US: The enigmatic Chimney Swift has declined by over 72 percent in the US as they lose their chimney habitat. If one is interested in the conservation of Chimney Swifts, here are some ideas: Provide a nesting habitat at your home a neighborhood swift tower could be a great Eagle Scout project hire a chimney sweep to cap your chimney in November, then reopen it in the spring in time for swift nesting. For larger buildings, consider the swifts that nest in chimneys before the chimneys are torn down.

Thursday, March 30

Friday, March 31

Saturday, April 1

Sunday, April 2

APRIL 2023

Sunday	Monday	Tuesday	Wednesday
Mar 26	Mar 27	Mar 28	Mar 29
2	3	4	5 Passover begins
9 Easter	10	11	12
16	18	19	20
24	25	26	27

Thursday	Friday	Saturday	Notes
Mar 30	Mar 31	Apr 1	
6	7	8	
13	14	15	
21	22	23	
28	29	30	

April 2023

April

M	T	W	T	F	S	S
					1	2
3	4	5	6	7	8	9
10	11	12	13	14	15	16
17	18	19	20	21	22	23
24	25	26	27	28	29	30

Monday, April 3

Tuesday, April 4

Wednesday, April 5 Passover Begins

Regional/Seasonal Birb Observe—Across the US: Male Red-winged Black-birds are unmistakable at feeders with their red and gold epaulets. The females are brown, heavily streaked with black, and have yellowing about their faces.

Thursday, April 6

Friday, April 7

Saturday, April 8

Easter Sunday, April 9

April 2023

FLIPPPIN' WILD BIRD 411: Butter butts. Yep. Yellow-rumped warblers are known affectionately as butter-butts. Their spring and fall migration can be great fun to observe, sweeping down and up the US in dense flocks. The Yellow-rumped Warbler's plumage is a splendid mix of bright yellow, charcoal gray and black, and bold white, with their butts of butter.

April

M	T	W	T	F	S	S
					1	2
3	4	5	6	7	8	9
10	11	12	13	14	15	16
17	18	19	20	21	22	23
24	25	26	27	28	29	30

Monday, April 10

_____
_____
_____
_____
_____
_____
_____
_____

Tuesday, April 11

_____
_____
_____
_____
_____
_____
_____
_____

Wednesday, April 12

_____
_____
_____
_____
_____
_____
_____

Beak tweak for the week: Jokes about butter are only marginally funny.

Regional/Seasonal Birb Observe—Eastern US: Black and white warblers are arriving to nest. They are also known as "Black and White Creepers," describing their appearance and behavior spot-on, hunting for insects in tree bark, similar to the nuthatch.
Across the US: The brilliant Yellow Warbler is a spring& summer visitor, nesting in shrub & woodland thickets. Listen for its "Sweet, sweet, sweet, I'm so sweet," call.

Thursday, April 13

Friday, April 14

Saturday, April 15

Sunday, April 16

April 2023

April

M	T	W	T	F	S	S
					1	2
3	4	5	6	7	8	9
10	11	12	13	14	15	16
17	18	19	20	21	22	23
24	25	26	27	28	29	30

Monday, April 17

_____
_____
_____
_____
_____
_____
_____

Tuesday, April 18

_____
_____
_____
_____
_____
_____
_____

Wednesday, April 19

_____
_____
_____
_____
_____

_____

<u>**Beak tweak for the week:**</u> I went to buy some camouflage pants, but I could not find any.

<u>Regional/Seasonal Birb Observe</u>—Western US: In arid and desert environments, the Ash-throated Flycatcher nests for breeding in March through August.

Eastern US: A Flycatcher, the Eastern Phoebe makes its home in the Spring and summer while it nests and raises its young. Listen for the fee-bee call around bridges and under the eaves of old buildings.

In 1804, the Eastern Phoebe became the first bird banded in North America, with John James Audubon applying the silver-thread bird ID.

Thursday, April 20

_____
_____
_____
_____
_____
_____
_____
_____

Friday, April 21

_____
_____
_____
_____
_____
_____
_____
_____

Saturday, April 22

_____
_____
_____
_____
_____
_____
_____
_____

Sunday, April 23

_____
_____
_____
_____
_____
_____
_____
_____

April 2023

April

M	T	W	T	F	S	S
					1	2
3	4	5	6	7	8	9
10	11	12	13	14	15	16
17	18	19	20	21	22	23
24	25	26	27	28	29	30

Monday, April 24

_____
_____
_____
_____
_____
_____
_____

Tuesday, April 25

_____
_____
_____
_____
_____
_____
_____

Wednesday, April 26

_____
_____
_____
_____
_____
_____

Beak tweak for the week: A knight carried a sword made of cheese. It was a very sharp cheddar.

Regional/Seasonal Birb Observe—California: The brave Rufous Hummingbird will spend spring traversing California on their migratory journey. Full of bravado, they are known to chase off hummingbirds twice their size from hummingbird feeders. Rufous typically spends about two weeks in an area, re-nourishing, then continuing on its journey.

Across the US: Hummingbirds can be spotted at nectar flowers and feeders.

Thursday, April 27

_____
_____
_____
_____
_____
_____
_____

Friday, April 28

_____
_____
_____
_____
_____
_____
_____

Saturday, April 29

_____
_____
_____
_____
_____
_____
_____

Sunday, April 30

_____
_____
_____
_____
_____
_____
_____

MAY 2023

Sunday	Monday	Tuesday	Wednesday
Jun 30	1	2	3
7 Mother's Day	8	9	10
14	15	16	17
21	22	23	24
28	29 Memorial Day	30	31

Thursday	Friday	Saturday	Notes
4	5	6	
11	12	13	
18	19	20	
25	26	27	
Jun 1	Jun 2	Jun 3	

May 2023

Arctic Terns fly over 18,000 miles each year, from the Arctic to the Antarctic and back again. They are known to fly thousands of miles out of their way to take advantage of good flying weather, being experts at letting oceans breezes carry them for long distances.

May

M	T	W	T	F	S	S
1	2	3	4	5	6	7
8	9	10	11	12	13	14
15	16	17	18	19	20	21
22	23	24	25	26	27	28
29	30	31				

Monday, May 1

Tuesday, May 2

Wednesday, May 3

<u>Beak tweak for the week:</u> There is a GPS for birders. It has tern by tern directions.

<u>Regional/Seasonal Birb Observe</u>—Coastal North America: Arctic Terns fly along the coast in large numbers in their migratory journey. They will start appearing in April, their numbers at their greatest in May.

Thursday, May 4

_____
_____
_____
_____
_____
_____
_____
_____

Friday, May 5

_____
_____
_____
_____
_____
_____
_____
_____

Saturday, May 6

_____
_____
_____
_____
_____
_____
_____
_____

Sunday, May 7

_____
_____
_____
_____
_____
_____
_____
_____

May 2023

Doves mate for life and have a unique sleeping position, looking like feathered fluff balls.

May

M	T	W	T	F	S	S
1	2	3	4	5	6	7
8	9	10	11	12	13	14
15	16	17	18	19	20	21
22	23	24	25	26	27	28
29	30	31				

Monday, May 8

Tuesday, May 9

Wednesday, May 10

<u>**Beak tweak for the week**</u>: A pigeon put on some scuba gear, then it dove.

<u>Regional/Seasonal Birb Observe</u>—Across the US: Mourning Doves thrive in open areas. During the breeding season, three Mourning Doves may be spotted flying in a tight formation, one after another Typically, the bird in the lead is the male of a mated pair. The second bird is an unmated male chasing his rival, in hopes of winning the spot with the female. The third is the female of the mated pair, who apparently goes along to see who wins.

Thursday, May 11

Friday, May 12

Saturday, May 13

Sunday, May 14

May 2023

A flock of hummingbirds is known as a charm, glittering, shimmer, tune, bouquet, or hover.

May

M	T	W	T	F	S	S
1	2	3	4	5	6	7
8	9	10	11	12	13	14
15	16	17	18	19	20	21
22	23	24	25	26	27	28
29	30	31				

Monday, May 15

_____
_____
_____
_____
_____
_____
_____
_____

Tuesday, May 16

_____
_____
_____
_____
_____
_____
_____
_____

Wednesday, May 17

_____
_____
_____
_____
_____
_____

Regional/Seasonal Birb Observe—Across the US: Spring migration can treat the observer to many different species of song birds. Get comfortable and patiently scan tree-tops with a pair of binoculars. Live in the moment and enjoy!

Thursday, May 18

Friday, May 19

Saturday, May 20

Sunday, May 21

May 2023

May

M	T	W	T	F	S	S
1	2	3	4	5	6	7
8	9	10	11	12	13	14
15	16	17	18	19	20	21
22	23	24	25	26	27	28
29	30	31				

Monday, May 22

Tuesday, May 23

Wednesday, May 24

<u>**Beak tweak for the week:**</u> What do you call a duck that can fix anything?   Duck tape.

<u>Regional/Seasonal Birb Observe</u>—Across the US: Lots of cute, fuzzy ducklings and goslings swimming with their mamas. I would love to know how successful you are at NOT smiling when you see baby ducklings safely toddling or swimming behind their mother.

Thursday, May 25

_____
_____
_____
_____
_____
_____
_____

Friday, May 26

_____
_____
_____
_____
_____
_____
_____

Saturday, May 27

_____
_____
_____
_____
_____
_____
_____

Sunday, May 28

_____
_____
_____
_____
_____
_____
_____

May 2023

The female Baltimore Oriole can tie knots with plant fibers she uses to build her sturdy nest. These knots secure the twigs, grasses and other materials she has woven into this strong basket.

May

M	T	W	T	F	S	S
1	2	3	4	5	6	7
8	9	10	11	12	13	14
15	16	17	18	19	20	21
22	23	24	25	26	27	28
29	30	31				

Mon, May 29 Memorial Day

Tuesday, May 30

Wednesday, May 31

<u>Regional/Seasonal Birb Observe</u>—Across the Mid-Atlantic, Great Plains and Eastern US: the colorful Baltimore Orioles can be spied at treetops and feeders stocked with oranges and grape jelly. They spend spring and early summer in these areas for breeding.

Thursday, June 1

Friday, June 2

Saturday, June 3

Sunday, June 4

JUNE 2023

Sunday	Monday	Tuesday	Wednesday
May 28	May 29	May 30	May 31
4	5	6	7
11	12	13	14
18 Father's Day	19	20	21
25	26	27	28

Thursday	Friday	Saturday	Notes
1	2	3	
8	9	10	
15	16	17	
22	23	24	
29	30	Jul 1	

June 2023

June

M	T	W	T	F	S	S
			1	2	3	4
5	6	7	8	9	10	11
12	13	14	15	16	17	18
19	20	21	22	23	24	25
26	27	28	29	30		

Monday, June 5

_____
_____
_____
_____
_____
_____
_____

Tuesday, June 6

_____
_____
_____
_____
_____
_____
_____

Wednesday, June 7

_____
_____
_____
_____
_____
_____

Bird tweak for the week: What bird can lift the most?
A crane.

<u>Regional/Seasonal Birb Observe</u>—Eastern US: Scarlet & Summer Tanagers spend spring & summer high in the treetops. With a bit of patient scouting of the tree canopy in dense woods, one may spot brilliant reds of these breath-taking birds. Westerm US: The Black-headed Grosbeak is a treat all around with colorful cinnamon, black and white coloring, and a beautiful song. They enjoy just about any environment, from backyards, to wooded areas to desert. They have strong beaks for cracking seeds & may be attracted to sunflower seeds in your feeder.

Thursday, June 8

Friday, June 9

Saturday, June 10

Sunday, June 11

June 2023

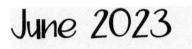

FLIPPIN' WILD BIRD 411: WHAT a longtongue you have! Flickers, Sapsuckers, and Woodpeckers are all in the Woodpecker family. They are all bestowed with incredibly long tongues which wrap up behind their brains extend down into the forehead, being part of the structures which protect their brain from concussions while drumming.

June

M	T	W	T	F	S	S
			1	2	3	4
5	6	7	8	9	10	11
12	13	14	15	16	17	18
19	20	21	22	23	24	25
26	27	28	29	30		

Monday, June 12

_____
_____
_____
_____
_____
_____
_____
_____

Tuesday, June 13

_____
_____
_____
_____
_____
_____
_____
_____

Wednesday, June 14

_____
_____
_____
_____
_____
_____

_____
_____

<u>Regional/Seasonal Birb Observe</u>—Across most of the US: Northern Flickers can be heard drumming year-round, except pockets of Texas and Southern California, where they only spend the winter. Eastern Northern Flickers have a red whisker next to their beaks, the Western variety have a black whisker. Betchya didn't know they needed to shave!

Thursday, June 15

_____
_____
_____
_____
_____
_____
_____
_____

Friday, June 16

_____
_____
_____
_____
_____
_____
_____
_____

Saturday, June 17

_____
_____
_____
_____
_____
_____
_____
_____

Sunday, June 18 Father's Day

_____
_____
_____
_____
_____
_____
_____
_____

June 2023

June

M	T	W	T	F	S	S
			1	2	3	4
5	6	7	8	9	10	11
12	13	14	15	16	17	18
19	20	21	22	23	24	25
26	27	28	29	30		

Monday, June 19

Tuesday, June 20

Wednesday, June 21

Bird tweak for the week: What's smarter than a talking parrot?   A spelling bee!

Regional/Seasonal Birb Observe—All over the US: Robins will not be ignored. They start singing earlier and earlier to beat the morning traffic, singing their iconic ,"Cheer up, cheer up, cheerily," well before dawn.

—

Thursday, June 22

Friday, June 23

Saturday, June 24

Sunday, June 25

June 2023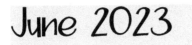

FLIPPPIN' WILD BIRD 411: Pigeons recognize human faces.
Pigeons can find their way home, even if flipping blindfolded (I imagine the pigeon was not happy about this). They can navigate by sensing the earth's magnetic fields, and possibly also by using sound and smell.

June

M	T	W	T	F	S	S
			1	2	3	4
5	6	7	8	9	10	11
12	13	14	15	16	17	18
19	20	21	22	23	24	25
26	27	28	29	30		

Monday, June 26

_____
_____
_____
_____
_____
_____
_____
_____

Tuesday, June 27

_____
_____
_____
_____
_____
_____
_____
_____

Wednesday, June 28

_____
_____
_____
_____
_____
_____
_____

_____

Bird tweak for the week: This pigeon became a dictator. It all started as a coo.

Regional/Seasonal Birb Observe—All over the US: Pigeons enjoy grain, dried corn and peas, and sorghum—if you now find yourself with more of an appreciation for this intlligent game bird. Some cities have ordinances against feeding pigeons, be aware of your local pigeon laws.

Thursday, June 29

Friday, June 30

Saturday, July 1

Sunday, July 2

JULY 2023

Sunday	Monday	Tuesday	Wednesday
Jun 26	Jun 26	jun 27	2jun 28
2	3	4 Independence Day	5
9	10	11	12
16	17	18	19
23 30	24 31	25	26

Thursday	Friday	Saturday	Notes
jun 29	Jun 30	1	
6	7	8	
13	14	15	
20	21	22	
27	28	29	

July 2023

FLIPPIN' WILD BIRD **411**: Flocks of larks are also known as a bevy, exaltation, ascension, and happiness.

How can you not smile?

July

M	T	W	T	F	S	S
					1	2
3	4	5	6	7	8	9
10	11	12	13	14	15	16
17	18	19	20	21	22	23
24	25	26	27	28	29	30
31						

Monday, July 3

_____
_____
_____
_____
_____
_____
_____
_____

Tuesday, July 4 Independence Day

_____
_____
_____
_____
_____
_____
_____
_____

Wednesday, July 5

_____
_____
_____
_____
_____
_____
_____

<u>**Beak tweak for the week:**</u> what do you call a duck who loves fireworks?   A fire quacker!

<u>Regional/Seasonal Birb Observe</u>—Across the US: Horned Larks live year-round on open ground: Airports, golf courses, prairies, large yards, plowed fields, beaches, lake flats. you get the idea. Look for what appear to be moving clods of dirt with little faces.

Horned Larks sing a delicate, musical song often as early as an hour and a half before sunrise.

Thursday, July 6

Friday, July 7

Saturday, July 8

Sunday, July 9

July 2023

July

M	T	W	T	F	S	S
					1	2
3	4	5	6	7	8	9
10	11	12	13	14	15	16
17	18	19	20	21	22	23
24	25	26	27	28	29	30
31						

Monday, July 10

Tuesday, July 11

Wednesday, July 12

Regional/Seasonal Birb Observe—Great plains and eastern US: Catbirds can be spotted and definitely heard during spring and summer, their breeding season. Listen for them imitating the calls of other birds and the mewing of a kitten or cat.

Thursday, July 13

_____
_____
_____
_____
_____
_____
_____
_____

Friday, July 14

_____
_____
_____
_____
_____
_____
_____

Saturday, July 15

_____
_____
_____
_____
_____
_____
_____

Sunday, July 16

_____
_____
_____
_____
_____
_____
_____

July 2023

July

M	T	W	T	F	S	S
					1	2
3	4	5	6	7	8	9
10	11	12	13	14	15	16
17	18	19	20	21	22	23
24	25	26	27	28	29	30
31						

Monday, July 17

_____

_____

_____

_____

_____

_____

_____

Tuesday, July 18

_____

_____

_____

_____

_____

_____

_____

Wednesday, July 19

_____

_____

_____

_____

_____

_____

_____

Regional/Seasonal Birb Observe—Across the US: Some birds may attempt a July brood, whether it be due to a broken heart, an unsuccessful spring brood, or a desire for a second brood. Keep your eyes peeled for those little nestlings.

Thursday, July 20

Friday, July 21

Saturday, July 22

Sunday, July 23

July 2023

July

M	T	W	T	F	S	S
					1	2
3	4	5	6	7	8	9
10	11	12	13	14	15	16
17	18	19	20	21	22	23
24	25	26	27	28	29	30
31						

Monday, July 24

Tuesday, July 25

Wednesday, July 26

<u>Beak tweak for the week:</u> If you hold a happy hour for catbirds and cowbirds, would you be herding catbirds?

<u>Regional/Seasonal Birb Observe</u>—Across the US: Goldfinches are fluttering about backyard feeders in gilted abundance.
House finches adorn feeders and branches with their raspberry-colored heads and chests bobbing about.
In the fall, male goldfinches molt their brilliant gold coloring and look very much like the females.

Thursday, July 27

Friday, July 28

Saturday, July 29

Sunday, July 30

July 2023

July

M	T	W	T	F	S	S
					1	2
3	4	5	6	7	8	9
10	11	12	13	14	15	16
17	18	19	20	21	22	23
24	25	26	27	28	29	30
31						

Monday, July 31

_____
_____
_____
_____
_____
_____
_____
_____

Tuesday, August 1

_____
_____
_____
_____
_____
_____
_____
_____

Wednesday, August 2

_____
_____
_____
_____
_____
_____

_____
_____

Regional/Seasonal Birb Observe—Across the US: The morning bird chorus has quieted as baby birds are fledging and songbirds form flocks rather than defend territories. When birds are in molt, they bring less attention to themsleves as their flight will not be as swift.

Thursday, August 3

Friday, July 4

Saturday, August 5

Sunday, August 6

AUGUST 2023

Sunday	Monday	Tuesday	Wednesday
30 July	31 July	1	2
6	7	8	9
13	14	15	16
20	21	22	23
27	28	29	30

Thursday	Friday	Saturday	Notes
3	4	5	
10	11	12	
17	18	19	
24	25	26	
31	1 Sep	2 Sep	

August 2023

August

M	T	W	T	F	S	S
	1	2	3	4	5	6
7	8	9	10	11	12	13
14	15	16	17	18	19	20
21	22	23	24	25	26	27
28	29	30	31			

Monday, August 7

Tuesday, August 8

Wednesday, August 9

<u>Regional/Seasonal Birb Observe</u>—The eastern US is treated to the beautiful Northern Cardinals year-round. Males are the quintessential bright red, females are a beautiful brown with red variations and crest.

Western US has the Red Crossbill in abundant numbers in conifer forests and groves, also year-round.

Thursday, August 10

Friday, August 11

Saturday, August 12

Sunday, August 13

August 2023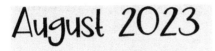

August

M	T	W	T	F	S	S
	1	2	3	4	5	6
7	8	9	10	11	12	13
14	15	16	17	18	19	20
21	22	23	24	25	26	27
28	29	30	31			

Monday, August 14

_____
_____
_____
_____
_____
_____
_____

Tuesday, August 15

_____
_____
_____
_____
_____
_____
_____

Wednesday, August 16

_____
_____
_____
_____
_____

<u>Regional/Seasonal Birb Observe</u>—Across the US year-round: Colorful Blue Jays can be heard communicating specific messages to each other across the neighborhood and woods, if you listen to the changes in the nature of their calls and the apparent context.

Across the US: Red-tailed hawks soar through the skies.

Thursday, August 17

_____
_____
_____
_____
_____
_____
_____
_____

Friday, August 18

_____
_____
_____
_____
_____
_____
_____

Saturday, August 19

_____
_____
_____
_____
_____
_____
_____

Sunday, August 20

_____
_____
_____
_____
_____
_____
_____

August 2023

Faster than a speeding train! Peregrine Falcons, when dropping through the sky toward their prey with closed wings, have been calculated to achieve speeds of 238 mph!

August

M	T	W	T	F	S	S
	1	2	3	4	5	6
7	8	9	10	11	12	13
14	15	16	17	18	19	20
21	22	23	24	25	26	27
28	29	30	31			

Monday, August 21

Tuesday, August 22

Wednesday, August 23

Beak tweak for the week: Chewbacca locked the keys in the Millenium Falcon. It was a wookie mistake.

Regional/Seasonal Birb Observe—Across the US: Peregrine Falcons are migrating. Almost eradicated from the Eastern US, their numbers are rebounding through conservation efforts. They can be found living on top of city buildings, in river valleys, mountain ranges and coastlines._

Thursday, August 24

Friday, August 25

Saturday, August 26

Sunday, August 27

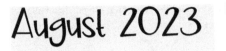
August 2023

FLIPPPIN' WILD BIRD 411: Crows create & use tools. They will drop hard-to-break nuts in front of moving cars then retrieve them between traffic, and drop stones into containers to get to deep water. Crows are known to hold vigil over their dead. It is thought they are trying to figure out how that crow died, as to avoid it themselves. Some avian scientist advise to move a dead crow after dark, so their murder does not witness you doing touching their flock-member.

August

M	T	W	T	F	S	S
	1	2	3	4	5	6
7	8	9	10	11	12	13
14	15	16	17	18	19	20
21	22	23	24	25	26	27
28	29	30	31			

Monday, August 28

Tuesday, August 29

Wednesday, August 30

Regional/Seasonal Birb Observe—Across the US: It's molting season Bald-headed birds, especially Blue Jays and Cardinals, may be noted if they have a "catastrophic molt" during molting. They are still healthy and will sport a full head of feathers and crest in about a month.

Thursday, August 31

_____
_____
_____
_____
_____
_____
_____
_____
_____

Friday, September 1

_____
_____
_____
_____
_____
_____
_____
_____
_____

Saturday, September 2

_____
_____
_____
_____
_____
_____
_____
_____

Sunday, September 3

_____
_____
_____
_____
_____
_____
_____
_____

SEPTEMBER 2023

Sunday	Monday	Tuesday	Wednesday
27 Aug	28 Aug	29 Aug	30 Aug
3	4	5	6
10	11	12	13
17	18	19	20
24	25	26	27

Thursday	Friday	Saturday	Notes
31 Aug	1	2	
7	8	9	
14	15	16	
21	22	23	
28	29	30	

September 2023

FLIPPPIN' WILD BIRD 411: Vultures have stomach acid so corrosive that they can digest carcasses infected with anthrax. Vultures' heads are bald so carrion is more easily cleansed away.

September

M	T	W	T	F	S	S
				1	2	3
4	5	6	7	8	9	10
11	12	13	14	15	16	17
18	19	20	21	22	23	24
25	26	27	28	29	30	

Monday, September 4 - Labor Day

Tuesday, September 5

Wednesday, September 6

Regional/Seasonal Birb Observe—Across the US: Nighthawks are heading toward the Mississppi flyway to migrate to their wintering grounds. This common flyway for Nighthawks has just been recently discovered. Some Nighthawks have flown over 1800 miles due east from British Columbia to get onto the Missisippi Flyway.

Thursday, September 7

Friday, September 8

Saturday, September 9

Sunday, September 10

September 2023

FLIPPPIN' WILD BIRD 411: Most birds migrate at night. The stars and the moon aid birds' navigation. The atmosphere is more stable, making it easier to maintain a steady course, which is especially helpful for smaller birds. Cool nighttime temperatures also help to boost endurance.

September

M	T	W	T	F	S	S
				1	2	3
4	5	6	7	8	9	10
11	12	13	14	15	16	17
18	19	20	21	22	23	24
25	26	27	28	29	30	

Monday, September 11

_____
_____
_____
_____
_____
_____
_____
_____

Tuesday, September 12

_____
_____
_____
_____
_____
_____
_____
_____

Wednesday, September 13

_____
_____
_____
_____
_____
_____
_____

Beak tweak for the week: I recently got back together with a light switch. We have been on and off for years.

Regional/Seasonal Birb Observe—Flipping off those indoor and outdoor light switches, midnight to 6a, spring and fall, helps to keep our hard-flying avian friends on course, by decreasing confusing light sources.

Thursday, September 14

Friday, September 15

Saturday, September 16

Sunday, September 17

September 2023

FLIPPPIN' WILD BIRD 411:
A hummingbird's heart beats up to 1,260 times a minute during migration, and its wings flap 15 to 80 times A SECOND. Hummingbirds fly alone when they migrate - not in flocks.

September

M	T	W	T	F	S	S
				1	2	3
4	5	6	7	8	9	10
11	12	13	14	15	16	17
18	19	20	21	22	23	24
25	26	27	28	29	30	

Monday, September 18

Tuesday, September 19

Wednesday, September 20

Regional/Seasonal Birb Observe—Across the US: Starting in late August,
the hummingbirds observed in yards at flowers and feeders or wild
nectar sources often change over daily.
Along the northern Gulf Coast, people provide an abundance of sugar-
water feeders and nectar flowers to help hummingbirds prepare for the
perilous 18-24 hour non-stop solo flight across the Gulf of Mexico.

Thursday, September 21

Friday, September 22

Saturday, September 23

Sunday, September 24

September 2023

FLIPPPIN' WILD BIRD 411: Get your mind out of the flippin' gutter. If you thought "Woodcock" was a funny name, this round fluffball has several nicknames: timberdoodle, night partridge, big-eye, bogsucker, and mudbat. The American Woodcock is one of the slowest flying birds It can stay airborne at just 5 miles per hour.

September

M	T	W	T	F	S	S
				1	2	3
4	5	6	7	8	9	10
11	12	13	14	15	16	17
18	19	20	21	22	23	24
25	26	27	28	29	30	

Monday, September 25

Tuesday, September 26

Wednesday, September 27

<u>Beak tweak for the week:</u> Quail, quail, quail, what do we have here?

<u>Regional/Seasonal Birb Observe</u>—Eastern US: In spring and summer, the plump, brown American Woodcock, bogsucker, enjoys the forest floors of the Eastern US as it searches the rich soil with its long bill for earthworms. The Woodcock remains in the south year-round.
Westen US: The round, plump Mountain Quail has a dramatic plume, which resembles an exclamation point. They are easier to hear than see.

Thursday, September 28

Friday, September 29

Saturday, September 30

Sunday, October 1

OCTOBER 2023

Sunday	Monday	Tuesday	Wednesday
1	2	3	4
8	9	10	11
15	16	17	18
22	23	24	25
29	30	31	1 Nov

Thursday	Friday	Saturday	Notes
5	6	7	
12	13	14	
19	20	21	
26	27	28	
2 Nov	3 Nov	4 Nov	

October 2023

October

M	T	W	T	F	S	S
						1
2	3	4	5	6	7	8
9	10	11	12	13	14	15
16	17	18	19	20	21	22
23	24	25	26	27	28	29
30	31					

Monday, October 2

_____
_____
_____
_____
_____
_____

Tuesday, October 3

_____
_____
_____
_____
_____
_____

Wednesday, October 4

_____
_____
_____
_____
_____

_____

Beak tweak for the week: My friend told me a joke about a raven. It was in Poe taste.

<u>Regional/Seasonal Birb Observe</u>—Relax, don't rake the leaves. Instead, put your feet up, knowing you have left a bounty for birdies of insects for food, retain essential water, shelter from bad weather and predators, materials for nest-building.
Ground feeders like the Dark-eyed Junco, Cardinals, and Doves will appreciate that you did not tidy the yard.

Thursday, October 5

_____
_____
_____
_____
_____
_____
_____

Friday, October 6

_____
_____
_____
_____
_____
_____
_____

Saturday, October 7

_____
_____
_____
_____
_____
_____
_____

Sunday, October 8

_____
_____
_____
_____
_____
_____
_____

October 2023

October

M	T	W	T	F	S	S
						1
2	3	4	5	6	7	8
9	10	11	12	13	14	15
16	17	18	19	20	21	22
23	24	25	26	27	28	29
30	31					

Monday, October 9

_____
_____
_____
_____
_____
_____
_____

Tuesday, October 10

_____
_____
_____
_____
_____
_____
_____

Wednesday, October 11

_____
_____
_____
_____
_____
_____

_____

<u>**Beak tweak for the week:**</u> My pet raven, Poe, started coughing. I thought it was Corvid-19, then the bird flu away. I guess I will see him nevermore.

<u>Regional/Seasonal Birb Observe</u>—Western and Northern US: Ravens live from the outskirts of towns (particularly landfills) to foothill forests or scrub and the deep woods of mountains.
Look for a long-tailed black bird flying with easy, graceful wingbeats on large wings.
Ravens are making a comeback in the Eastern US.

Thursday, October 12

Friday, October 13

Saturday, October 14

Sunday, October 15

October 2023

October

M	T	W	T	F	S	S
						1
2	3	4	5	6	7	8
9	10	11	12	13	14	15
16	17	18	19	20	21	22
23	24	25	26	27	28	29
30	31					

Monday, October 16

Tuesday, October 17

Wednesday, October 18

Regional/Seasonal Birb Observe—Western US, Year-Round: The entertaining and gregarious Black-billed Magpie often sits atop fence posts and road signs. They can be amusing, imitating other animal sounds and human speech.

Thursday, October 19

Friday, October 20

Saturday, October 21

Sunday, October 22

October 2023

October

M	T	W	T	F	S	S
						1
2	3	4	5	6	7	8
9	10	11	12	13	14	15
16	17	18	19	20	21	22
23	24	25	26	27	28	29
30	31					

Monday, October 23

_____
_____
_____
_____
_____
_____
_____

Tuesday, October 24

_____
_____
_____
_____
_____
_____
_____

Wednesday, October 25

_____
_____
_____
_____
_____
_____

Beak tweak for the week: What do you call it when a raven marries a crow? A conspiracy to commit to murder.

Regional/Seasonal Birb Observe—Across the US year-round: American Crows are abundant.
Across the Western US and in some pockets of the Northern and Eastern US: Ravens make their home year-round but are expanding more and more into areas of the US from where they had long disappeared.

Thursday, October 26

Friday, October 27

Saturday, October 28

Sunday, October 29

October 2023

October

M	T	W	T	F	S	S
						1
2	3	4	5	6	7	8
9	10	11	12	13	14	15
16	17	18	19	20	21	22
23	24	25	26	27	28	29
30	31					

Monday, October 30

Tuesday, October 31

Wednesday, November 1

<u>**Beak tweak for the week:**</u> What helps roosting crows stick together for warmth? Velcrow.

<u>Regional/Seasonal Birb Observe</u>—Across the US: As the weather gets cooler, crows gather in large colonies to roost together. The sight can be spectacular and eerie, like something from Alfred Hitchcock's "The Birds."

Thursday, November 2

Friday, November 3

Saturday, November 4

Sunday, November 5

NOVEMBER 2023

Sunday	Monday	Tuesday	Wednesday
Oct 29	Oct 30	Oct 31 Halloween	1
5	6	7	8
12	13	14	15
19	20	21	22
26	27	28	29

Thursday	Friday	Saturday	Notes
2	3	4	
9	10	11 Veterans Day	
16	17	18	
23 Thanksgiving	24	25	
30	Dec 1	Dec 2	

November 2023

Mini-me's! Downy Woodpeckers look like miniature versions of the Hairy Woodpecker (I challenge you to say "Hairy Woodpecker" without cracking a smile). Other than both belonging to the woodpecker family and being extremely cute, they are not closely related.

November

M	T	W	T	F	S	S
		1	2	3	4	5
6	7	8	9	10	11	12
13	14	15	16	17	18	19
20	21	22	23	24	25	26
27	28	29	30			

Monday, November 6

Tuesday, November 7

Wednesday, November 8

<u>**Beak tweak for the week:**</u> what is a bunch of crows gathering money called?   Crow funding.

<u>Regional/Seasonal Birb Observe</u>—Across the US year-round: Both the Downy and Hairy Woodpeckers can be heard drumming. It is fun to see them near each other with their striking black and white coloring. Almost exact copies of each other, but different sizes.

Thursday, November 9

Friday, November 10

Saturday, November 11

Sunday, November 12

November 2023

November

M	T	W	T	F	S	S
		1	2	3	4	5
6	7	8	9	10	11	12
13	14	15	16	17	18	19
20	21	22	23	24	25	26
27	28	29	30			

Monday, November 13

_____
_____
_____
_____
_____
_____

Tuesday, November 14

_____
_____
_____
_____
_____
_____

Wednesday, November 15

_____
_____
_____
_____
_____
_____

<u>Beak tweak for the week:</u> Turkeys often use fowl language when they're mad.

<u>Regional/Seasonal Birb Observe—US</u>: Pine Siskins and Goldfinches are frequent visitors to backyard bird feeders in the winter.

Across the US, year-round: Goldfinches are abundant   males lose their bright gold plumage in the winter. near woods if there are berry or nut-bearing trees planted.

Thursday, November 16

_____
_____
_____
_____
_____
_____
_____

Friday, November 17

_____
_____
_____
_____
_____
_____
_____

Saturday, November 18

_____
_____
_____
_____
_____
_____
_____

Sunday, November 19

_____
_____
_____
_____
_____
_____
_____

November 2023

FLIPPPIN' WILD BIRD 411:
That is a bunch of crap!
Male Wild Turkeys drop their
poop in a J shape, and female
turkeys create a curlycue with their leavings. Turkeys often use fowl language
when they're mad.

November

M	T	W	T	F	S	S
		1	2	3	4	5
6	7	8	9	10	11	12
13	14	15	16	17	18	19
20	21	22	23	24	25	26
27	28	29	30			

Monday, November 20

Tuesday, November 21

Wednesday, November 22

Regional/Seasonal Birb Observe—Across the lower 2/3 of the US: The Ruby-crowned kinglets are settling in for the winter. They are tiny, olive-colored birds males sport an often obscured ruby crown. Watch for their frequent wing flicking.

Across the US: House and Purple Finches show off their beautiful and similar coloring. The red House Finch lives across the US, except a small central corridor. The Purple Finch winters in the central and Eastern US.

Thursday, November 23 Thanksgiving

Friday, November 24

Saturday, November 25

Sunday, November 26

November 2023

November

M	T	W	T	F	S	S
		1	2	3	4	5
6	7	8	9	10	11	12
13	14	15	16	17	18	19
20	21	22	23	24	25	26
27	28	29	30			

Monday, November 27

Tuesday, November 28

Wednesday, November 29

Regional/Seasonal Birb Observe—Across the US, year-round, except a few pockets in the Northwest, Wild Turkeys can be attracted to yards near woods if there are berry or nut-bearing trees in supply.

Thursday, November 30

Friday, December 1

Saturday, December 2

Sunday, December 3

DECEMBER 2023

Sunday	Monday	Tuesday	Wednesday
26 Nov	27 Nov	28 Nov	29 Nov
3	4	5	6
10	11	12	13
17	18	19	20
24 Christmas Eve / New Year's Eve / 31	25 Christmas	26 Kwanza begins	27

Thursday	Friday	Saturday	Notes
30 Nov	1	2	
7 Hanukkah begins	8	9	
14	15	16	
21	22	23	
28	29	30	

December 2023

Mourning Doves can store an enormous amount of seed in their crop to digest later.

The largest known record is 17,200 bluegrass seeds in a single crop.

December

M	T	W	T	F	S	S
				1	2	3
4	5	6	7	8	9	10
11	12	13	14	15	16	17
18	19	20	21	22	23	24
25	26	27	28	29	30	31

Monday, December 4

Tuesday, December 5

Wednesday, December 6

<u>Regional/Seasonal Birb Observe-</u>Across the Northern US: Some male Mourning Doves do not migrate to the warmer Southern US and instead brave the cold winters to have an advantage in establishing a territory for spring mating.

Thursday, December 7

Friday, December 8

Saturday, December 9

Sunday, December 10

December 2023

FLIPPPIN' WILD BIRD 411:
Magpies could write a mystery novel with some of the names for groups of magpies: Charm congregation, murder, and mischief!

December

M	T	W	T	F	S	S
				1	2	3
4	5	6	7	8	9	10
11	12	13	14	15	16	17
18	19	20	21	22	23	24
25	26	27	28	29	30	31

Monday, December 11

_____
_____
_____
_____
_____
_____
_____

Tuesday, December 12

_____
_____
_____
_____
_____
_____
_____

Wednesday, December 13

_____
_____
_____
_____
_____
_____

<u>Beak tweak for the week:</u> what is an owl's favorite kind of book?   A hoo-dun-it.

<u>Regional/Seasonal Birb Observe</u>—Northwestern US, year-round: Magpies can be found at the tops of trees or fence posts, loud and proud, to be seen and heard.
Eastern US, year-round: The Woodthrush is heard but not seen with a unique, flute-like call, where the Woodthrush can harmonize with itself.

Thursday, December 14

_____
_____
_____
_____
_____
_____
_____

Friday, December 15

_____
_____
_____
_____
_____
_____
_____

Saturday, December 16

_____
_____
_____
_____
_____
_____
_____

Sunday, December 17

_____
_____
_____
_____
_____
_____
_____

December 2023

Hawk owls can hear their prey in under 12 inches of snow.

December

M	T	W	T	F	S	S
				1	2	3
4	5	6	7	8	9	10
11	12	13	14	15	16	17
18	19	20	21	22	23	24
25	26	27	28	29	30	31

Monday, December 18

_____
_____
_____
_____
_____
_____

Tuesday, December 19

_____
_____
_____
_____
_____
_____

Wednesday, December 20

_____
_____
_____
_____
_____

<u>Regional/Seasonal Birb Observe—</u>Across the US: December and January are great times to look for owls.

Trees that overlook an open area are ideal. Some clues to find a tree with a roost: owl calls, regurgitated indigestible prey hair and bones (aka owl pellets) at the foot of a tree, the movement of their distinctive outlines. It may take patience and perseverance, but it will be fun to watch the owl family grow once you locate a brooding couple and may provide for some fantastic winter memories.

Thursday, December 21

Friday, December 22

Saturday, December 23

Sunday, Dec 24 Christmas Eve

December 2023

Chickadees secret seeds away in numerous places to eat later and can remember over a thousand hiding places. In the spring, Chickadees feed each of their young about 350 catepillars a day!

December

M	T	W	T	F	S	S
				1	2	3
4	5	6	7	8	9	10
11	12	13	14	15	16	17
18	19	20	21	22	23	24
25	26	27	28	29	30	31

Monday, Dec 25 Christmas Day

_____
_____
_____
_____
_____
_____
_____
_____

Tuesday, December 26 Kwanza begins

_____
_____
_____
_____
_____
_____
_____
_____

Wednesday, December 27

_____
_____
_____
_____
_____
_____

Regional/Seasonal Birb Observe—Northern US Year-round: Black-capped Chickadees spread their cuteness abundantly.
Southeast US: The Carolina Chickadee flits about backyard feeders and woodlands.
Western US: The Mounatin Chickadees hang upside-down from their perches in dry everygreens to pluck bugs and berries.

Thursday, December 28

Friday, December 29

Saturday, December 30

Sunday, Dec 31 New Year's Eve

JANUARY 2024

Sunday	Monday	Tuesday	Wednesday
Dec 31 New Year's Eve	1 New Year's Day	2	3
7	8	9	10
14	15 Martin Luther King Day	16	17
21	22	23	24
28	29	30	31

Thursday	Friday	Saturday	Notes
4	5	6	
11	12	13	
18	19	20	
25	26	27	
Feb 1	Feb 2	Feb 3	

January 2024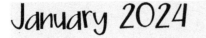

Some monikers for a flock of doves are: bevy, cote, flight, dules, pitying, piteousness.

The iconic 1-13 rising notes of a dove's cooo is made courting, waiting for a mate to return or flushing from a nest. The whistling sound made when they take-off is from a notched 7th primary wing feather.

January						
Mon	Tue	Wed	Thu	Fri	Sat	Sun
1	2	3	4	5	6	7
8	9	10	11	12	13	14
15	16	17	18	19	20	21
22	23	24	25	26	27	28
29	30	31				

Monday, January 1 New Year

_____
_____
_____
_____
_____
_____
_____

Tuesday, January 2

_____
_____
_____
_____
_____
_____
_____

Wednesday, January 3

_____
_____
_____
_____
_____
_____

_____

Beak tweak for the week: The dove went to college to study egg-onomics.

Regional/Seasonal Birb Observe—Across the US:Mourning Doves are not fans of bugs and spiders. They are grainivores. It is easy to attract Mourning Doves to your back yard or balcony with sunflower seeds, nyger, safflower, cracked corn, and peanuts.

Thursday, January 4

_____
_____
_____
_____
_____
_____
_____

Friday, January 5

_____
_____
_____
_____
_____
_____
_____
_____

Saturday, January 6

_____
_____
_____
_____
_____
_____
_____

Sunday, January 7

_____
_____
_____
_____
_____
_____
_____

January 2024

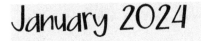

FLIPPIN' WILD BIRD 411: A group of Waxwings is collectively known as an "ear-full" and a "museum" of waxwings. Red, waxy secretions found on the wingtips of waxwings give them their name.

January						
Mon	Tue	Wed	Thu	Fri	Sat	Sun
1	2	3	4	5	6	7
8	9	10	11	12	13	14
15	16	17	18	19	20	21
22	23	24	25	26	27	28
29	30	31				

Monday, January 8

_____
_____
_____
_____
_____
_____
_____

Tuesday, January 9

_____
_____
_____
_____
_____
_____
_____

Wednesday, January 10

_____
_____
_____
_____
_____
_____

<u>Beak tweak for the week:</u> The emu who was taller than his friends was ostrichsized.

<u>Regional/Seasonal Birb Observe</u>—Across most of the US: During cold nights and bad weather Chickadees will roost alone in any little pocket or crevice they can find: trees, cracks in buildings, roosting pockets or bird boxes.

Thursday, January 11

_____
_____
_____
_____
_____
_____
_____

Friday, January 12

_____
_____
_____
_____
_____
_____
_____

Saturday, January 13

_____
_____
_____
_____
_____
_____
_____

Sunday, January 14

_____
_____
_____
_____
_____
_____
_____

January 2024

Owls' ears are offset. They hear something with their left ear before they hear it with their right. This helps with locating prey.

January						
Mon	Tue	Wed	Thu	Fri	Sat	Sun
1	2	3	4	5	6	7
8	9	10	11	12	13	14
15	16	17	18	19	20	21
22	23	24	25	26	27	28
29	30	31				

Mon, January 15
Martin Luther King Day

_____
_____
_____
_____
_____
_____
_____

Tuesday, January 16

_____
_____
_____
_____
_____
_____
_____

Wednesday, January 17

_____
_____
_____
_____
_____
_____

<u>**Beak tweak for the week:**</u> What do you call a funny chicken A comedi-hen.

<u>Regional/Seasonal Birb Observe</u>—Across the US, in cold areas: Cardinals roost together in conifers on cold winter nights and in bad weather

Thursday, January 18

_____
_____
_____
_____
_____
_____
_____
_____

Friday, January 19

_____
_____
_____
_____
_____
_____
_____
_____

Saturday, January 20

_____
_____
_____
_____
_____
_____
_____
_____
_____

Sunday, January 21

_____
_____
_____
_____
_____
_____
_____
_____

January 2024

Owls have three eyelids: an upper eyelid, an lower lid and a inner-most lid to help keep their eyes moistened.

January						
Mon	Tue	Wed	Thu	Fri	Sat	Sun
1	2	3	4	5	6	7
8	9	10	11	12	13	14
15	16	17	18	19	20	21
22	23	24	25	26	27	28
29	30	31				

Monday, January 22

_____
_____
_____
_____
_____
_____
_____

Tuesday, January 23

_____
_____
_____
_____
_____
_____
_____

Wednesday, January 24

_____
_____
_____
_____
_____
_____

<u>Beak tweak for the week</u>: The "Chicken Dance" is poultry in motion.

<u>Regional/Seasonal Birb Observe</u>—Central and Eastern US: Blue Jays live year-round. One can enjoy observing their teamwork.
Northwest: Blue Jays can entertain observers during the Fall and Winter. Only 1 10 of Blue Jays were found with remains of eggs or other birds in their stomachs, dispelling the belief that such is typical food for the Jay.

Thursday, January 25

_____

_____

_____

_____

_____

_____

_____

Friday, January 26

_____

_____

_____

_____

_____

_____

_____

Saturday, January 27

_____

_____

_____

_____

_____

_____

_____

Sunday, January 28

_____

_____

_____

_____

_____

_____

_____

January 2024

January						
Mon	Tue	Wed	Thu	Fri	Sat	Sun
1	2	3	4	5	6	7
8	9	10	11	12	13	14
15	16	17	18	19	20	21
22	23	24	25	26	27	28
29	30	31				

Monday, January 29

_____
_____
_____
_____
_____
_____
_____

Tuesday, January 30

_____
_____
_____
_____
_____
_____
_____

Wednesday, January 31

_____
_____
_____
_____
_____
_____

Beak tweak for the week: What do you call a parrot that just flew away? A polygon.

Regional/Seasonal Birb Observe—Across the US: Incredibly adorable Downy Woodpeckers inhabit backyards across the US in all seasons. In the winter, they can be attracted to backyards with suet and nuts. The Hairy Woodpecker looks like a bigger version of the Downy Woodpecker.

Notes for 2024

NOTES

NOTES

NOTES

NOTES

NOTES

NOTES

NOTES

NOTES

NOTES

NOTES

NOTES

NOTES

NOTES

NOTES

NOTES

NOTES

NOTES

NOTES

NOTES

Dear Fellow Bird Enjoyers -

Thank you for taking a chance on this planner. My hope is you found some bird-inspired delight to add a bit of fun to your days. I would LOVE to hear about it!

The bird information in this planner was researched through these sources:
The Cornell University Ornithology Lab AllAboutBirds.org
The Cornell University Ornithology Lab FeederWatch.org
The Audobon Society at Audobon.org
The American Bird Conservancy at abcbirds.org/birds
The Spruce at TheSpruce.com

This "wild about birds" planner creator currently makes monthly donatiosns to:
The Audobon Society
Cornell University Ornithology Lab
American Bird Conservancy.

If this planner does well, I have promised my backyard birds I would buy them more food and increase my contributions to these wonderful organizations.

Thank you -

Cardinal Bliss

CardinalBlissJournals@gmail.com

CARDINAL BLISS
Planners•Journals•Coloring Books